SAVE THE DRAMA FOR YOUR MAMA!

A LEADER'S GUIDE TO ORGANIZATIONAL ACCOUNTABILITY

SHERI L. MACKEY

ALSO BY SHERI L. MACKEY:

52 LEADERSHIP TRUTHS TO LIVE BY

VIRTUAL SUCCESS:
HOW TO BUILD HIGH PERFORMING VIRTUAL TEAMS

DESTINATIONS:
YOUR GUIDE TO SETTING & ACHIEVING MEANINGFUL GOALS

Acknowlegments

I would like to say thank you to Steve Mackey,
who is my partner in life,
as well as my strategic thinking partner

Stephen and Savannah Mackey,
Who make me smile every day and
give me the space to write

Matt Miller,
who teaches kids how to
"Save The Drama For Your Mama"

Kim Renga,
Who is my Editor and my friend

Ellie Kay,
Who is a wonderful friend and mentor

CONTENTS

INTRODUCTION

Good leaders are always in demand. But what happens when a good leader, or even a great leader, is distracted with organizational drama that inhibits employees from giving their best and impedes organizational success? What happens when objectives are not met because organizational drama impacts *our* ability to get things done? What happens when *we* spend more time putting out fires than focusing on achieving results? We experience it every day, yet organizational drama and how it detracts from our ability to achieve results is seldom, if ever, discussed. We have a cancer in organizations that has the power to:

- » **Decrease productivity**
- » **Contribute to missed deadlines**
- » **Erode trust and morale**
- » **Impact job performance**
- » **Cause conflict, missed opportunities and misinformation to flourish**
- » **Create fear**

> » **Produce falsely raised expectations**
> » **Entrench "toxic" work environments**

If this is true (and we all know it is), don't we, as leaders, have a responsibility to take an active role and manage the environment to the best of our ability? Most of us would agree, if on nothing else, that we have a responsibility to our organizations to facilitate the best results possible within the parameters we're given. So why do we accept people causing drama that inhibits us from achieving what we're capable of? Often it's because:

1. We are unsure of what to do about it

2. We are uncomfortable confronting the guilty

3. We do not acknowledge this as a pervasive problem

By embracing **inaction, we** have become the problem. This short, easy to read guide will provide some common sense ways to manage the challenge of drama within your organization. It will allow you, as a responsible leader, to take charge and minimize the drama in your organization.

If you are a leader (formal or informal) that is looking for a toolkit to help you manage change and navigate drama within your organization, keep reading. Whether you are trying to implement personal accountability, stem gossip, or manage expectations, this book will provide practical tips and tactics to manage the drama in your organization—large or small.

Develop these skills and you will become the highly respected leader you were meant to be!

1

PERSONAL ACCOUNTABILITY

"If you could kick the person in the pants responsible for most of your trouble, you wouldn't sit for a month."
—THEODORE ROOSEVELT

We've all experienced workplace drama in one form or another. It can be unpleasant, irritating, and disruptive—often preventing organizations from effectively meeting their goals. As a leader, you are responsible for maintaining a productive, drama-free workplace. You rely on *people* to do their jobs and successfully achieve results. Because you work with people to get things done, you're likely to experience drama in the workplace. It can sometimes feel like an experience similar to the television show *Super Nanny*—the kids (your organization) are spoiled and unruly, and you are the "Nanny"—responsible for teaching the foundational skills leading to both personal and organizational success. However, in the workplace (just as within dysfunctional families) gossip, complaining, and backstabbing lead to full-blown negativity resulting in increased absenteeism and turnover, amongst other things. How you manage the drama within your organization will have a significant impact on your ultimate ability to succeed.

It may feel personal at times, but as the "Nanny", it's your job to get the "children" back in line—ensuring they learn and engage in appropriate behaviors that create positive results for the organization.

We'll explore several ideas—hopefully providing you, the leader, with a toolkit to ensure you are in a position to eliminate (or at least drastically reduce) disruptive behavior in your area of responsibility. If you successfully manage drama, you are much more likely to see the positive results you desire.

Promoting personal accountability is a key component to getting trouble-makers under control. However, this can be extremely challenging. Irresponsible thinking, and a lack of accountability, is equal to drama in the workplace. It manifests itself as complaining and excuse making—and probably causes you to unnecessarily spend your time putting out fires. The reason employees participate in blaming, complaining, backstabbing and excuse-making is because it lessens the pain and discomfort of taking personal responsibility for their part in the disruption.

When you step in to fix the problem for an individual (or team) before they've made a valid attempt at independent resolution, they continue to respond from a victim mentality instead of an empowered and responsible mindset. They come to expect you to rescue them with increasing frequency. If you are spending excess time putting out fires instead of developing accountable employees, you're inevitably wasting time, energy and resources that could be spent on generating positive results.

Putting boundaries and systems in place for dealing with issues and challenges that employees may encounter is a key component to building an accountable and reliable workforce across an organization. We're not talking about Human Resource issues—we're specifically dealing with discontent between individuals (or amongst team members) that is not of an egregious nature.

An "open door policy" often sounds good, however, if you're working in a drama- infested environment, you may want to reconsider this policy.

Instead of an open door at any time, you can set office hours for open and honest discussion—with strict parameters. Anyone coming through your door must meet specific criteria if they have an issue or challenge. They must:

» Have a brief, yet clear, synopsis of the situation
» Understand how the situation impacts productivity, customer service, teamwork and/or the bottom line
» Always come with initial possibilities or ideas to resolve the matter

This lets everyone in the organization know you are serious about hearing their issues and challenges. It also lets them know you're *very* serious about expecting them to think through the situation and be prepared to help themselves before you're willing to engage the problem.

Whether it's complaining, negative attitudes or gossiping—workplace drama hampers productivity, affecting both organizational and personal effectiveness. Employees need to clearly and concisely understand that *they* are responsible for finding ways to change an unproductive situation, or accept it as the norm—anything else is just drama.

Are you unintentionally enabling drama in your organization?

2

GOSSIP IN THE WORKPLACE

"Strong minds discuss ideas, average minds discuss events, weak minds discuss people."

—SOCRATES

Gossip is as old as humanity itself. If you have drama in the workplace, you more than likely have gossip. It's found in nearly every work environment—these conspiratorial conversations are usually unverified, unsubstantiated, and occasionally... unseemly. Gossip is the type of chatter that appears as harmless speculation or good-natured teasing, but if left unchecked, has the potential to severely impact your ability to generate positive business results. Leaders need to recognize that gossip has a profound effect on their bottom line and not having a strategy to handle it could be a recipe for disaster.

Gossip may sound like a harmless, unavoidable by-product of corporate life, but left unchecked, rumor-mongering wreaks havoc on company morale and efficiency. A negative work environment is a less productive work environment. Gossip creates an uncomfortable atmosphere—not only for the person the gossip is about, but for everyone in the workplace.

Gossip can often be likened to the old childhood game of *Telephone*, where one person starts the spread of information and by the time it reaches the last person, it has evolved and changed into something entirely different. Some gossip may have truth to it, while other information carried on the gossip relay may be false. Either way, gossip should be avoided since it is a harmful means of communication.

Just in case you haven't given it a lot of thought, here are just a few destructive outcomes resulting from gossip in the workplace:

   » Wasted time and lost productivity
   » Severe erosion of trust and morale

» Hurt feelings and the possibility of reprisals
» Miscommunication leading to conflict, missed opportunities or misinformation
» Heightened fear or falsely raised expectations
» A "toxic" work environment

Now that you understand the severity of gossip, what can you do about it? First, you need to understand you are not likely to completely eliminate it. However, you also need to understand how an organization deals with habitual gossip can be the difference between growing and thriving... or disintegrating from within. Understanding the effect it has on achieving your organization's goals and objectives, your focus should be to limit gossip to the greatest possible extent. Below are some tips for controlling gossip in the workplace:

Establish Consequences:

Include a policy regarding gossip in the employee handbook that clearly defines the organization's stance on gossip and the ramifications it has for the company. It should also detail the consequences for those who consistently participate in this type of behavior.

Improve Communication:

Whether you are in a position to influence your company's HR Policies or not, you *can* develop an internal communications plan for your area of responsibility. Speak regularly with employees regarding the happenings within your organization. Gossip tends to occur when there's a vacuum of information. In the absence of frequent communication from their leader, people speculate or circulate rumors. Through openness about workplace issues and keeping everyone better informed, you can remove the need to create false information to fill the information gap. After all, gossip doesn't tend to go very far if the answer to *"Have you heard the latest?"* is always *"Yes, I have"*.

Be Responsible And Responsive:

Gossip can't exist without someone to tell it to. Explain to your employees if they are not the object of the gossip but they are listening, responding or passing along the information—they *are* participating in gossip. You need to make it clear that even the simple act of listening to gossip is a bad idea.

Promote Group Discussions:

Incorporate employee-driven group discussions and expectations about gossiping. This gives employees permission to hold each other mutually accountable for having a "gossip-free" workplace.

Go On The Offensive:

Confront the person who's gossiping. Ask the individual why they believe they should spread this information and what they'll personally gain from it. A strong offense is often the best defense against gossip. Tell the guilty party that you are calling in the person who's the object of the gossip to clarify the information... *and do it* while they're sitting there! This is a sure way to stop gossip in its track. Most gossips shy away from the prospect of directly repeating their rumors to the person referred to.

Be Proactive:

Tell the offender you're aware of the inappropriate behavior. Describe how it results in mistrust across the organization. Incorporate the (potential) impact of the behavior, and suggest how it will influence upcoming performance evaluations. For many, the likelihood of negative personal outcomes results in immediate change.

It's important for gossips to realize the toxic effect their behavior has on them, their coworkers, and the organization as a whole. When they stop, it means the team has taken on forthrightness and honesty in its communications, dealing head-on with issues through the person who has the ability to do something about it. This allows for teamwork, trust, communication—and therefore, extraordinary results.

What Are You Doing To Ensure Gossip Doesn't Sabotage Your Organization?

3

MANAGING EXPECTATIONS

"People rise and fall to meet your level of expectations. If you express skepticism and doubt in others, they will return your lack of confidence with mediocrity. But if you believe in them and expect them to do well, they will go the extra mile trying to do their best."

—JOHN C. MAXWELL

You can bet that if you don't set and manage expectations, drama invites itself in for an extended visit. When people don't know or understand the expectations you have of them, they create their own... which do not align across the organization. Disagreements and controversy ensue, causing chaos that distracts from driving positive results. While setting and managing expectations may seem time consuming, the cost (in time, effort and drama) of not doing so far exceeds that of encouraging personal responsibility through clearly letting people know what you expect of them.

As a leader, before you can hold others accountable for outcomes, you have to let them know what success looks like and what you expect to see as a result of their efforts. If everyone knows the expectations, the focus is on driving for results and monitoring against set standards. The benefit of setting and managing expectations is twofold:

1. **Clear, concise expectations drive action and decisions.**
2. **Explicit expectations are a primary driver of success.**

If you fail to create an environment where expectations are well understood and respected by those who work for you (and with you), you are highly unlikely to develop a high-performing organization... or deliver strong, sustainable business results.

Expectations are like the rules in the board game *Sorry!* When everyone knows the "rules" or "expectations", some may try and cheat, but the other players will hold the cheater accountable. When no one knows the rules it's impossible to be accountable, much less hold anyone else accountable... to anything. Organizations are no different—if you want your players to know how to play to win and hold others accountable, you are responsible for setting and managing expectations.

When setting expectations, consider these four principles:

1. Clarity

Expectations should focus on outcomes, not activities. Leaders often make the mistake of attempting to direct the process, rather than focusing on the desired outcome. As a leader, you should be responsible for identifying the goal, while the employee (or the team) is responsible for deciding how to meet or exceed expectations.

2. Relevance

Relevance helps define the "why" of what's expected. If employees have complete understanding of the importance of what they're asked to deliver, they'll be more committed to the result because they see how it fits into the big picture, as well as how their efforts impact the company.

3. Simplicity

Simplicity creates a sense of grounding for both individuals and teams. If you identify what's expected in simple, straight-forward terms, there is an explicit understanding of what is expected.

4. Consistency

After setting expectations, you must maintain a consistent approach to managing them so they are applicable to most situations. This facilitates a sense of unity and equality, and bolsters morale across the organization.

Now, let's consider three important components of expectations:

Setting Expectations

Set concise, clear and realistic expectations so people know what to expect and feel they can achieve success with sustainable effort. A leader's responsibility is to set employees up for success by engaging them in the process. People tend to cooperate much better when they understand and are committed to how you manage and what you really expect of them.

Monitoring Expectations

The truth is, you can't manage expectations unless you monitor them. In order to successfully monitor expectations, you need to engage both individuals and the team. More importantly, you need to hear and understand what you're being told and how it affects your organization. Monitoring enables you to assess progress and assist if unexpected roadblocks emerge. Explicit monitoring (not micromanaging) indicates that goals are important to you as a leader and that you're vested in achieving results alongside your people.

Influencing Expectations

Once you have clearly and concisely defined expectations and engaged your people, it's time to flex your influencing muscles to ensure every last person on your team is bought in and aligned with individual, team, and organizational goals.

Expectations are difficult to control and impossible to turn off. Everybody has them and if you, as a leader, are not explicit in communicating your expectations, there's a significant probability you may not produce the results *you* are expected to deliver. Expectations drive performance and establish benchmarks for success.

Your organization relies on your expertise, and it's up to you to help everyone within your sphere of influence understand what you need to generate great outcomes. Managing expectations gives you the power to control the environment (to the extent that it is possible) and guide people down the path toward delivering exceptional results.

Have you set clear and concise expectations for your organization?

4

THE CHALLENGE OF CHANGE

"Never doubt that a small group of thoughtful, committed citizens can change the world. Indeed, it is the only thing that ever has."

—MARGARET MEAD

Change is inevitable. However, you have a choice as to whether you control change or let change control you—creating unnecessary drama!

Leaders need the ability to present a unified vision and convey support if they expect their people to embrace change. Perceived indifference leads to a rapid demise of the change effort. As a leader facilitating change, make sure you provide:

» A clear vision for how the change will impact the individual, team, division, organization and the client base

» A firm commitment to change goals, while simultaneously accepting input on the details
» Specific, achievable objectives along with plans for achieving them (SMART Goals)
» A roadmap for success with realistic timelines, budgets, and owners
» A communication framework to support change adoption
» Opportunities for people to give feedback before, during and after the change

Admittedly, organizational change is complex, but we often make it harder on ourselves than it has to be. Just as in the board game *Clue*, it's easy to engage in false assumptions that can lead our people down the path of suspicion and drama—away from the truth and the possibility of an ultimate win. The result?

A whole lot of ambiguous thinking regarding the application of structured, human-focused, change within the organization.

Here are just a few examples of **false assumptions** we often fall victim to:

People Resist Change:

Actually, not always. People frequently seek out drastic changes in their lives and voluntarily embrace them. However, people do resist being forced to change. The way change is presented and managed impacts its success or failure far more than the change itself. Most of us respond far better to change when we comprehend a valid reason for it. Without solid justification, most people are likely to resist anyone who tries to force change upon them... and cause plenty of drama along the way.

Providing A Solution *Is* Fixing The Problem:

It's not. "Buy-in" suggests that a leader has defined the necessary change (or "the solution") and is now attempting to convince (or persuade) people to accept the change. This isn't a good strategy because, in most cases, the leader has made little effort to effectively define the problem for employees. *Of course* people resist change and create drama if they believe you are trying to fix something that's not broken—perception is 90% of reality! If you, as a leader, are trying to sell a solution to a problem that people aren't even aware of, is it any wonder they resist? Don't attempt to sell a solution before you have defined the problem. If people are aware there's a problem and have the opportunity to help solve it, they'll go to great lengths to support a change they perceive they are a part of.

As A Leader You Are An Exception To *The Golden Rule*—Treat Others As You Would Like To Be Treated

You're not. It's a fallacy to assume leaders are different than anyone else. We all have hearts and minds and want to be treated with respect and decency. Do you respond better to being told to change, or when people ask you to participate in change in response to a real problem? Just a reminder—you are **NOT** an exception to The Golden Rule!

Change isn't easy, but there's no reason for a change effort to be riddled with false assumptions and unnecessary drama—if it's well planned and potential issues are proactively addressed. If you work alongside your people to meet practical, achievable goals, you won't fail.

By making change processes transparent, encouraging open dialogue, and being receptive to constructive criticism, you'll help your people to accept change and will reap great rewards.

How do you keep from falling victim to false assumptions in your change efforts?

5

CHANGE IN A PRODUCTIVE CONTEXT

"Change is hard because people overestimate the value of what they have—and underestimate the value of what they may gain by giving that up."

—JAMES BELASCO

We've examined some common myths surrounding change management that have the potential to derail change efforts. Organizational change reminds me of the movie *Jumanji*. It involves a supernatural board-game that brings it's jungle world to life and puts the actual players in jeopardy of being maimed, or perhaps worse yet, caught in the drama forever! Sound familiar? It's a jungle out there, and if you want to avoid drama that could maim your change effort, not only do you need to dispel myths, but you also need to put solid game rules in place that will keep everyone on the same game board... and playing according to the same set of rules.

Here are some suggestions to foster effective change:

Acknowledge The 300 Pound Rhino In The Room

Don't try and covertly institute change—silence, denial and mislabeling always make the situation worse. Call the rhino, well... a rhino—let your people know there are uncomfortable changes taking place. Demonstrate your commitment by asking your opinion leaders for their ideas as to how to go about the change and actually implement the best contributions. If you want your people to embrace change, they must have the chance to voice concerns and offer input. Effective change management includes listening carefully to concerns and fears—perceived, imagined, or legitimate—that could become barriers. Open communication provides valuable insight, letting you lay the foundations for effective change.

Provide Clear, Concise Communications

Even the most dedicated employees want to know how change will personally affect them. It's critical to provide clear and accurate information to the furthest possible extent. Whether they say it or not, people will naturally have the following questions or concerns:

- » How the change will affect *me*?
- » What will *I* need to do differently?
- » Will *I* need additional skills to be successful... if so, how will *I* learn them?
- » Will the change affect *my* position/role?
- » Will *I* be moved or eliminated?
- » How will *I* know if the change is good for *me*?

Answer these questions. Openly communicate. People more easily accept change if they know what to expect. Managing expectations is tricky, but it's vital to success.

Make the case for change—provide a clear and convincing rationale for the change and support it with sound evidence and supporting information regarding the personal impact to each and every person. Let those affected know about the proposed change in advance. Advise everyone of the honest implications for individuals, teams, functions, and organizations.

Get People Involved In Change

Encourage your opinion leaders to understand and participate in the change to gain their support. If you can get your opinion leaders on board, chances are others will follow. Communicate the changes (and the anticipated benefits for your organization as well as for individuals) to team members, colleagues, and senior managers in order to gain both broad and deep support. Make every effort to let people know how the change will benefit them—everyone loves to know WIIFM (What's in it for me).

Provide people the opportunity to openly comment on the proposed change and help in the planning. It's absolutely critical that everyone knows and understands the importance of their role in the change. The more they understand and are included in change, the more they will own it!

Develop & Communicate A Detailed Plan:

At minimum, your plan should include the 6 w's:

1. *Who* will be affected by the change:

Detail who will be involved, the process for choosing team members, and what the individual roles will be. Make sure you brief everyone affected by the change on their role in the change process and the possible impact to their area, as well as all other critical roles. Consistently validate understanding and encourage them to ask questions.

2. *What,* specifically, is the change that needs to happen:

Announce the change itself, as well as the objectives of the change—providing as many details as possible.

3. *Why* does change need to happen:

What is the challenge or problem making change necessary? *Why* is it important? Explain how and why the current challenge is impacting the organization and the potential for a better future based on the proposed change.

4. *When* will the change take place:

Provide an anticipated timeline, including a starting point and finish-line, with key milestones along the way. If you don't know, provide as much information as you have.

5. *Where* will the change take place:

Be clear as to which functions, departments, organizations or campuses will be affected.

6. *How* will the change happen:

How will the change be implemented and monitored? How will resources be allocated? How will people know the change has been successful? Fully describe the process to evaluate each stage of the change. Provide a date and time for the next update.

The morale and productivity of the entire workforce can be destroyed if there's a lack of planning and communication on the part of ill-equipped leaders. Even if you're charismatic and have a knack for verbal delivery, communications can easily careen out of control and cause drama ... or worse, if not carefully managed. To ensure consistency, leverage both verbal and written communications. People absorb and understand information in different ways. Verbal messages make communications personable and believable. Written communications reinforce what you've said and ensure everyone has identical information, while presenting irrefutable facts and allowing time for reflection and preparation.

7. Keep It Positive

When change isn't progressing the way you had envisioned, communicate why things aren't going smoothly and a plan of action for getting things moving in the right direction, always focusing on maintaining people's morale and motivation.

There is almost always someone who resists change and causes drama, making life difficult for you and others. Negativism can sabotage change acceptance. Identify those individuals not open to the change. Understand their concerns. Help them to see how the change will make their lives easier. If you can convert your greatest opponents into change evangelists, you may exceed your own expectations.

Change isn't easy, but there's no reason for a change effort to cause unnecessary drama—if it's well planned and potential issues are proactively addressed. If you work alongside your people to meet practical, achievable goals, you're not likely to fail. By making change processes transparent, encouraging open dialogue, and being receptive to constructive criticism, you'll be a positive role model, helping your people to accept change that reaps great rewards for everyone.

Are you doing everything you can to ensure change is successful in your organization?

6

A CALL TO ACTION

I trust you have enjoyed this book. As you go forward, I wish you success and suggest that you keep in mind that it is essential that you realize that you must...

"Be the change that you wish to see in the world."

—MAHATMA GANDHI

If you do not utilize the tools you have been given, *you* are responsible for the drama that takes place in your organization. You have a distinct opportunity to take action and make a real difference in your work environment and in people's lives.

My challenge to you:

In the name of forging a productive and success-ful organization—use the tools you have been given to go forth and conquer the drama in your organization today!

ABOUT THE AUTHOR

MEET SHERI, THE GLOBAL COACH...

 F ew people have influenced global leadership more than Sheri L. Mackey. Known as **"The Global Coach"**, Sheri is a highly sought-after author, speaker, and executive coach with a unique perspective on global leadership, intercultural communications and organizational change in the international marketplace.

Sheri is also the President and CEO of Luminosity Global Consulting Group—a strategic leadership coaching and consulting firm providing a full range of services focused on developing exceptional executives across boundaries and borders.

For over 20 years, Ms. Mackey's partnerships with Fortune 500 companies have resulted in organization-wide initiatives that facilitate exceptional business results on a worldwide basis. Sheri's global enterprise expertise makes her uniquely qualified to inspire, as well as enable, high potential leaders to drive for extreme organizational results.

Ms. Mackey is universally characterized by both colleagues and clients as one of the most insightful, powerful, and compassionate individuals in global business today. Living and working in diverse countries throughout most of her life, Sheri is one of the most knowledgeable and influential global leadership experts in the world and is respected for her exceptional work in international leadership and management.

Sheri received her MBA in International Management from the University of Cambridge, as well as her B.Sc. in Psychology from the University of Maryland. She also completed her post-graduate work in International Coaching and is a certified coach with the International Coach Federation.

Having a strong belief in social responsibility, Sheri serves on several Not-For-Profit Board of Directors, leads both foreign and local Mission trips to help the less fortunate and mentors at-risk teenage girls.

For more detailed information on Sheri or Luminosity Global Consulting Group, please contact info@luminosityglobal.com.

SHERI MACKEY THE GLOBAL COACH

LEADERSHIP ACROSS BOUNDARIES & BORDERS

CONNECT WITH SHERI:

Twitter:	LuminosityGlobe
Facebook:	Sheri L. Mackey
LinkedIn:	Sheri Mackey
Leadership Blog:	www.sherimackey.com